Making Cheese

Marie Hartley and Joan Ingilby

Smith Settle

First published in 1997 by
Smith Settle Ltd
Ilkley Road
Otley
West Yorkshire
LS21 3JP

ISBN 1 85825 083 8

British Library Cataloguing-in-Publication data:
A catalogue record for this book is available from the British Library.

Set in Monotype Plantin

Designed, printed and bound by
SMITH SETTLE
Ilkley Road, Otley, West Yorkshire LS21 3JP

Introduction

Reputable historians of cheese suggest that it was made from the milk of sheep and goats in prehistoric times. This is likely but it is guesswork. It was certainly made by the Romano-British as surviving utensils for cheese-making indicate. We are on firmer ground when we reach monastic times. In 1145 a group of Cistercian monks founded Fors Abbey (the forerunner of Jervaulx) at Dale Grange on the margin of the Forest of Wensleydale. The remote site was not approved of, and about 1150, to justify their choice, the monks issued an inventory of their stock and provisions, which included cheese, presumably made of ewes' milk. Thus documentary evidence of cheese-making in Wensleydale is recorded in the twelfth century.

Also *The Fountains Abbey Lease Book* (edited by D J H Michelmore and published by the Yorkshire Archaeological Society), gives fascinating glimpses of cheese-making and butter-making in the Middle Ages. The monks of Fountains Abbey leased their granges and lodges to tenants, some of whom had charge of a few in Nidderdale described as 'dary-houses'. Herds belonging to these numbered from sixty to twenty cows with bulls and followers, and by the terms of the leases the milk made into cheese and butter in summertime supplied the abbey. A condition stipulated that all should be 'housewyffly handeled'. The annual milk yield from one cow was reckoned at 40 gallons (whereas in 1800 it was 400 and in 1996 1,250). These products had to be delivered in early November to the cheese house at Fountains, which was in the charge of the 'maister', a monk. We read that in 1537 the 'daryhouse' at Burthawit in Nidderdale was contracted to despatch 80 stone of cheese and 40 stone of butter to the abbey. What a picture of dairy work on a large scale is conjured up, as well as the importance of cheese to the diet of the monks!

It is noticeable that the cheese was made from cows' not ewes' milk — a changeover that took place gradually. Sometimes the two seem to have been mixed to make cheese. As late as 1579 a witness in a lawsuit described how he used to buy cheese and butter at Stalling Busk near Semerwater, and had seen the 'wives' there milking their 'Kyne and Yeowes'.

After the Dissolution of the Monasteries, granges and lodges turned into hamlets and farms, and dairywork continued. In 1794 the trade in butter from Nidderdale and Dentdale was extolled. Butter was sent from Nidderdale via York to the London market (just as cheeses from the northern dales were sent to London by sea after Yarm Fair from Stockton). In 1780 Thomas Maude wrote of Wensleydale: 'The commodities of the valley for home and foreign consumption are fat cattle, horses, wool, butter, cheese, mittens, calamine and lead'. At a market for butter started at Hawes in 1878, 3,000 lbs were regularly sold. Wensleydale came into prominence when in the 1840s important cheese fairs were established at Leyburn, thus probably starting the name of Wensleydale for cheese. This is the general name, but is varied by Cotherstone, Ribblesdale, Coverdale and Swaledale for cheese made in those dales, all using a similar recipe. The pastoral nature of the Dales countryside, the limestone pastures, a plentiful rainfall, and the herby grass for feed for the cows make for rich milk.

In this and the last century, a few farms with large herds of cows took up cheese-making in a big way and attracted customers from all over the country. But mostly it was made in individual small farmhouse dairies, usually making cheeses weighing from 4 to 5 lbs and some 8 to 18 lbs. Even some with very few cows managed to make cheese. Factors from industrial towns came to buy it, or it was sold at fairs, or bartered at grocer's shops in return for provisions. Not all was well made. Two books *Dairy Farming* and *Practical Cheese-making* became bibles for the dairymaid, and as well classes were started conducted by advisers from the Department of Agriculture at Leeds University.

Cheese-making was on the whole women's work, occupying almost all day as the process involved intervals between each stage. In the old days the curdling agent was got by drying the stomach of a calf on two crossed sticks, boiling it, and using a piece as starter. Also cheeses were salted in brine. Towards the end of the last century, rennet for curdling became available, and cheese was dry-salted by adding salt to the curds — two important changes. Cheesemaking as in monastic times was summer work, when the cows calved and left their winter quarters to graze in the meadows.

The following is the standard recipe for Wensleydale cheese. First, milk from the night before is poured through a sieve into the cheese kettle, and the morning's milk added. Heat to 85° and add starter (rennet), half a teaspoon to four gallons of milk. Stir. Let stand for an hour, cover and keep warm. Cut it. Ladle the whey off gently, through muslin. Hang in the dairy in a muslin bag for 4 to 6 hours. Weigh the curds and crumble. Add salt (half an ounce to one pound of curds). Line the vat with muslin and crumble curds loosely into it. Put the sinker (lid) on. Place in the press and adjust pressure. Leave overnight. Take out and bandage. Store in the dairy or cheese room, turning twice at first, then once daily. The important sales of cheese took place in the autumn when the cheese had dried.

The most valuable item of equipment for cheese-making is the cheese kettle, especially when made of copper or brass. Cheese vats were well-made with wooden staves hooped with iron hoops. Formerly cheese presses were made of wood. Then, early in the last century, stone presses were installed in back kitchens, outdoor alcoves or little buildings of their own. Many have gone, but those that remain are impressive relics. They were superseded by cast-iron presses supplied by ironmongers who often had their name embossed on them. Cleanliness was essential. Utensils had to be scalded, and aired out of doors on the bink, a stone bench situated near the kitchen door.

One daughter of the family usually specialised in making butter, which requires a quantity of cream. Before separators arrived, cream was drawn off from milk left standing to set in large lead-lined vats kept on dairy shelves. Further equipment consisted of a churn, wooden bowls, butter prints, butter hands, weighing scales, a slate, and a butter worker if available. The early plunger or stand churn was worked by a pumping action; barrel and end-over-end churns came into use in the last century. Waides of Leeds are credited with the invention of the Victoria churn in about 1880. This varied in size from one holding 2 gallons of cream to one holding 35 (which had to be driven mechanically). For smaller quantities of butter there were table and glass churns.

After churning, the butter was washed with water three times, and came out 'pinhead'. Then it was 'clashed' in a butter bowl, or put in the butter worker to squeeze out the buttermilk. Salt was added and checked for taste, and after clashing again the butter was weighed into pounds, some round, some oblong, made with butter hands, and some formed into rolls, and left to stand. Then they were embossed with wooden hand-carved prints, with patterns specific to each farm, or dextrously patterned with the butter hands. Many are the stories of churning for hours in winter, because the butter had 'gone to sleep', and of the rock bottom prices prevailing at times. Making 30 lbs a week was usual, but one friend told us that she made 90 lbs at home and 70 lbs for her brother each week on one day.

When the railway came to Hawes in Wensleydale in 1878, and when dairies were opened from 1897 onwards, farmhouse cheesemaking heard its death knell. It ceased at the time of the Second World War. The sale of milk sent by train or collected by local dairies was advantageous in that it brought ready money to the farm, and the women were released from hard toil (although some regretted the loss of satisfying work). Large enterprising dairies now take most of the milk, and one or two make goats' and ewes' cheese. Only here and there may a farmer's wife make cheese for her family or friends. Cheesemaking has to be licensed.

In the 1960s, when cheese and butter-making had almost faded away, we were able to photograph Mrs P Metcalfe at Shoregill, Swaledale, and Mrs M Alderson at Angram, Swaledale, making cheese, and Mrs W Mason of Lodge Hall, Ribblesdale, and Miss E Alderson of Black Howe, upper Swaledale, making butter.

Photographic Acknowledgements

We wish to thank Mr F J Willis for the photograph on page 8; Mrs W H Nixon for that on page 10; and Mrs J Metcalfe for that on page 28.

Margaret Willis binding Wensleydale cheeses at Manor Farm, Carperby, Wensleydale, c1898. Here cheese was made on a large scale. They won championships for cheese at the London Dairy Show, and sold cheeses to Fortnum and Mason.

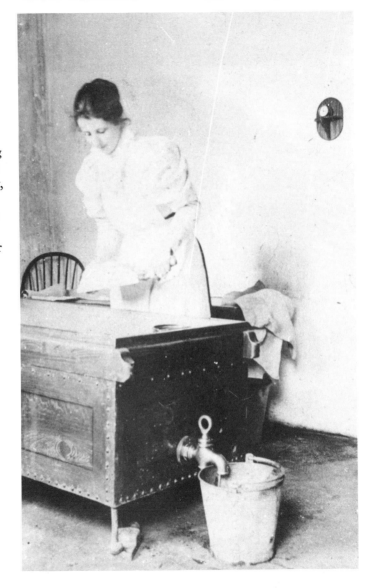

Mrs W Birkett of West Park, Cotherstone, making Cotherstone cheese. She is putting curds into a cheese vat ready for pressing. She sold cheese all over the country in the autumn. (1939)

The dairy at West Park, with rows of cheeses waiting to mature on traves —
wooden cheese shelves (1915).

Milk being heated to 85° over a fire in a cheese kettle hanging on a reckon. The kettle had to be lifted on and off by the farmer or farmhand.

Mrs P Metcalfe at Shoregill, Swaledale, making cheese.
She pours milk through a sieve into the cheese kettle.

She adds cheese rennet (one dessertspoon to twenty gallons of milk) and heats the milk to 85°.

The milk having been heated and curdled, she pours the curds into a large bowl, and leaves it to stand for one hour.

She cuts down the curds into small pieces with a curd breaker.

Putting the curds into a cloth for straining.

Then hang up in the cloth in the dairy for four hours. Note the stone dairy shelves, on which are weighing scales, a bottle of rennet and a separator.

Putting curds into a cheese vat.

With the sinker (lid) put on, the vat is placed in
the cheese press for twenty-four hours.

She sews the cheese in a calicoe bandage to preserve the shape,
and then stores it in the dairy or cheese room.

The utensils used — cheese kettle, sieve, cheese vat, bridge for sieve,
and cheese breaker — are put out to air on the bink.

Mrs M Alderson makes cheese at Angram, Swaledale. She is pouring milk through a sieve into the kettle from a backcan.

She adds cheese
rennet.

Ladling off the whey by pressing with a cloth. Then she hangs the curds in muslin in the dairy for at least four hours to strain. *(Right)* Breaking the curds and placing them in a cheese vat.

Adjusting the
pressure on the
cheese vat in the
iron cheese press.

Cheese drying on traves at a farm near Barnard Castle (1967).

An early type of cheese press made of wood from Thwaite, Swaledale, The bar was lowered on to the cheese vat by cranking the chain round the wooden wheel. Then a stone weight was suspended from a crook at the end of the bar.

An outdoor alcove filled with shelves for dairy utensils. The farmer brings in milk in a backcan, and his wife attends to a cheese press. (Date unknown.)

A typical last-century cheese press at Studfold, Ribblesdale.
Built in 1812 in an outdoor alcove, it cost £1 19s 6d.

A cheese press in the garden of West Mill, Askrigg, Wensleydale.
The stone sinks into a pit.

Two cheese presses at Hill Top Farm, Oxnop, Swaledale, with the stones sunk into pits. One was used up to about 1960 and both were in operation in the 1920s.

A cheese press in an ouside alcove at Spen House, Askrigg, Wensleydale. The stone is sunk in a pit. The scored circle and cross on a stone is where the vat was placed. All base stones of cheese presses had these for drainage.

Butter Prints

Stand or plunger butter-churns at the Dales Countryside Museum. Two are made of wooden staves, of which one is bound by ash bands, and the other by iron hoops. The other two are ceramic from Wensleydale.

Mrs W E Iceton demonstrates using the stand churn. The stick has a round wooden plunger at the bottom end, and is pumped up and down and swivelled in the hands. Churns like this were used to make butter in the Middle Ages

Mrs W Mason of Lodge Hall, Ribblesdale, churns cream in an end-over-end churn.

She clashes the
butter in a bowl
to remove the
buttermilk.

37

She rolls the butter in the bowl to make cone shapes for round pounds.

Weighing and making round pounds, finishing with a round butter-print.

Miss E Alderson, Black Howe, upper Swaledale, churns cream in a table churn.

Transferring the butter from the churn into a butter bowl.

Clashing to remove the buttermilk.

Weighing out the pounds.

Making up into long pounds and printing the top with a pattern with the butter hands.

Mrs W J Middleton of Dent squeezes out the buttermilk in a butter worker. The roller is wound up and down in the wooden trough seven times. It holds about twelve pounds.

Mrs L Simpson of Westfield, Nidderdale, rolls her butter on a board to make round pounds.

Butter markers have different patterns carved on them, so that each one distinguishes a particular dairy.